Crushing CREDIT CARD DEBT like a pro

Zero to Hero

Arthur Crandon LL.B.(Hons.) M.A.

Zero to Hero - Crushing Credit Card Debt like a pro

Copyright Arthur Crandon 2024

All rights reserved. No part of this book may be reproduced, stored in a retrieval system, or transmitted in any form or by any means—electronic, mechanical, photocopying, recording, or otherwise—without the prior written permission of the publisher, except for brief quotations in critical reviews or articles.

This is a work of fiction. Names, characters, places, and incidents are either the product of the author's imagination or used fictitiously. Any resemblance to actual persons, living or dead, events, or locales is entirely coincidental.

ISBN: 9798340981295

Cover design by Lynnie Ceniza
Interior design and formatting by Lynnie Ceniza
Published by Arthur Crandon Publishing
Visit our website: Arthurcrandon.co.uk

DISCLAIMER

The information provided in this book is for general informational purposes only. It does not constitute legal, financial, or professional advice. While every effort has been made to ensure accuracy, the author and publisher assume no responsibility for errors or omissions. Readers should consult with appropriate professionals for specific advice tailored to their individual circumstances.

First Edition: August 2024

BUILDING UP CREDIT CARD DEBT IS SO EASY THESE DAYS – YOU ARE ENCOURAGED TO DO IT – THEN MADE TO FEEL LIKE A CRIMINAL WHEN YOU STRUGGLE WITH PAYMENTS

YOU ARE NOT ALONE.

WE WILL HELP YOU TO RESTRUCTURE AND JOIN THE MILLIONS WHO HAVE REGAINED THEIR LIVES

CONTENTS

	Acknowledgments	i
1	Understanding Debt	1
2	Assessing your Situation	7
3	Creating a Repayment Strategy	13
4	Budgeting	17
5	Negotiating with Creditors	23
6	Emergency Fund	29
7	Frugal Habits	35
8	Extra Income	43
9	Strategies	47
10	Financial Discipline	53

This book will give you all the structure, the help, and the encouragement you need to get your life back on course.

1 UNDERSTANDIING DEBT

1. **Understanding Your Debt Landscape**

2. **What Is Credit Card Debt?**

   - **Definition**: Credit card debt is a type of unsecured liability incurred through revolving credit card loans. When you use your credit card to make purchases, you're essentially borrowing money from the card issuer.

- **How It Works**: You charge expenses to your card, and at the end of the billing cycle, you receive a statement with the total amount owed. You have the option to pay the full balance or make a minimum payment,

3. **Common Reasons People Accumulate Credit Card Debt**:

    - **Living Beyond Means**: Sometimes, we let our spending outpace our income. That fancy dinner, those concert tickets, and that spontaneous shopping spree—all on the card. Before you know it, the balance balloons.

    - **Emergency Expenses**: Unexpected medical bills, car repairs, or home emergencies can lead to credit card reliance. When life throws curveballs, the plastic often catches them.

- **Lack of Emergency Fund**: Without a safety net (like an emergency fund), people turn to credit cards when faced with unexpected costs.

- **Card Rewards Temptation**: Ah, the siren call of rewards points! We chase those miles, cash back, or discounts, but sometimes it leads us down the debt rabbit hole.

- **Multiple Cards**: Having too many cards can be like juggling flaming torches—eventually, one slips. Each card adds complexity, and managing them all can become overwhelming.

4. **The Impact of Interest Rates and Minimum Payments**:

   o **Minimum Payments**: These are the smallest amounts you're required to pay each month to keep your account in good standing. Paying only the minimum is like treading water—it keeps you afloat but doesn't get you anywhere. Plus, it's a slow crawl toward debt freedom.

   o **Interest Charges**: Credit card interest rates (APR) can be steep (usually 15% to 20% or more). When you make only the minimum payment, your unpaid balance accumulates interest. It's like a snowball rolling downhill: the more you owe, the more interest you pay. Transferring debt to 0% APR cards can temporarily halt interest charges.

- **Long-Term Consequences**: Paying just the minimum extends your repayment timeline. Look at your credit card bill—there's usually a "Minimum Payment Warning" that shows how long it'll take to pay off your balance if you stick to the minimum. Spoiler alert: It's a looong time. Paying more than the minimum shortens that period significantly.

Remember, credit cards can be powerful tools when used wisely. But like any superpower, they come with responsibilities.

2 ASSESSING Y0UR SITUATION

Let's break down each step to help you assess your financial situation effectively:

1. **Create Financial Goals**:

    o Start by setting clear financial goals. Why are you conducting this audit? What do you hope to achieve? Whether it's saving for a specific purchase, building an emergency fund, or paying off debt, having well-defined goals will guide your financial decisions[1]

- Ask yourself: What am I working toward? What matters most to me financially?

2. **Collect Financial Data**:

    - Gather all relevant financial information. This includes:

        - **Income**: Calculate how much money you earn each month. Consider all sources of income, such as your salary, side gigs, or rental income.

        - **Expenses**: Categorize your expenses. Track everything—from rent or mortgage payments to utility bills, groceries, entertainment, and discretionary spending. Use budgeting apps or create a financial calendar to stay organized.

- **Debts**: Understand your debt situation. List all outstanding debts, including credit card balances, loans, and any other obligations.

  o Knowing your net worth (assets minus liabilities) is also helpful. It gives you a snapshot of your overall financial health.

3. **Evaluate Your Budget**:

   o If you already have a budget, review it carefully. If not, create one. A budget helps you manage your cash flow effectively.

   o Look at the details of your income and expenses. Understand where your money is coming from and where it's going. Use banking and credit card apps—they provide real-time insights into your spending patterns.

- Ask yourself: Am I prioritizing the right things? Are there areas where I can cut back?

4. **Assess Your Debt Situation**:

    - Calculate your total credit card debt. Add up the balances on all your credit cards.
    - Consider using a credit card payoff calculator to estimate how long it will take to pay off your debt. You can adjust monthly payment amounts to see different scenarios.

    - Also, evaluate your credit utilization ratio. Divide your total credit card balances by your total credit limit and multiply by 100 to get the percentage. Aim for a low utilization rate to maintain a healthy credit score.

5. **Review Your Investments**:

    - If you have investments (such as retirement accounts or stocks), assess their performance. Are they aligned with your long-term goals?

- Consider diversification and risk tolerance. Adjust your investment strategy if needed.

6. **Update Your Financial Goals**:

    - Based on your findings, revisit your financial goals. Are they realistic? Do you need to adjust them?

    - Set specific, measurable targets. For example, aim to pay off a certain amount of debt by a particular date or save a specific sum for an emergency fund.

7. **Plan for the Future**:

    - Armed with this information, create an action plan. Prioritize paying off high-interest debt, building an emergency fund, and saving for retirement or other goals.

    - Automate savings and debt payments where possible. Consistency is key.

Remember, a personal finance audit is like shining a light on your financial habits—it helps you make informed decisions and take control of your money.

3 CREATING A REPAYMENT STRATEGY

Let's dive into some practical strategies for paying off debt. Whether you're dealing with credit cards, student loans, or other obligations, having a clear plan can make a significant difference. Here are several effective approaches:

1. **Debt Snowball Method**:

    o **What it is**: This method prioritizes your smallest debts first.

    o **How it works**: Pay the minimum on all your debts, but put extra money toward the smallest balance. Once that's paid off, move to the next smallest debt.

- **Why it works**: It provides quick wins and builds momentum as you eliminate smaller debts, which can be motivating.

2. **Debt Avalanche Approach**:

    - **What it is**: Focuses on high-interest debts.

    - **How it works**: Pay the minimum on all debts, but allocate extra funds to the debt with the highest interest rate. Once that's paid off, move to the next highest interest rate debt.

    - **Why it works**: Mathematically, it minimizes interest costs over time.

3. **Debt Consolidation**:

    - **What it is**: Combining multiple debts into a single loan or credit card.

- **How it works**: You'll have one monthly payment at a potentially lower interest rate.

- **Why it works**: Simplifies repayment and may reduce overall interest.

4. **Create a Detailed Budget**:

    - **What it is**: Tracking your income and expenses.

    - **How it works**: Identify necessary costs (like housing and utilities) and discretionary spending (like dining out or streaming services). Cut unnecessary expenses to free up funds for debt repayment.

    - **Why it works**: A budget keeps you on track and ensures bills are covered.

5. **Automate Your Payments**:

    - **What it is**: Set up automatic payments for your debts.

- **How it works**: Avoid late fees and ensure consistent progress.

- **Why it works**: Helps maintain discipline and prevents missed payments.

6. **Increase Your Income**:

    - **What it is**: Find ways to earn more money.

    - **How it works**: Side gigs, freelancing, or asking for a raise can boost your income.

    - **Why it works**: More income means more to put toward debt.

Remember, everyone's situation is unique. Choose a strategy that aligns with your financial goals, lifestyle, and preferences

4 BUDGETING

Let's dive into each step of budgeting, cutting expenses, and allocating funds toward debt repayment.

1. Develop a Realistic Budget

Creating a budget is like giving your money a roadmap—it helps you navigate toward your financial goals. Here's how to get started:

Step 1: Calculate Your After-Tax Income

Your after-tax income is the money you take home after deductions like taxes, retirement contributions, and health insurance. If you have automatic deductions, add those back in to get a true picture of your available funds.

Step 2: Choose a Budgeting System

There are various budgeting systems, so pick one that suits your style:

- **Envelope System**: Allocate cash into envelopes for different spending categories (groceries, entertainment, etc.). When an envelope is empty, you stop spending in that category.

- **Zero-Based Budget**: Assign every dollar a purpose. Your income minus expenses should equal zero.

Step 3: Track Your Progress

Record your spending—use apps, spreadsheets, or even a good old pen and paper. Pay attention to where your money goes. If you spot overspending, consider cutting those costs. Redirect those funds toward debt repayment or savings.

Step 4: Automate Savings

Make it easy on yourself! Set up automatic transfers from your paycheck to emergency savings, investment accounts, and retirement funds. Having an accountability partner or joining an online support group can also keep you on track.

Step 5: Regularly Review and Adjust

Life changes, and so should your budget. Revisit it periodically—maybe once a quarter—to ensure it aligns with your current situation.

2. Identify Areas to Cut Back on Spending

Now, let's trim those expenses without sacrificing too much joy:

1. Track Your Spending

Start by understanding where your money is going. Use a budgeting app, a spreadsheet, or even a simple notebook. Sometimes we're surprised by how much we spend in certain categories!

2. Cook at Home More Often

Eating out can be a budget buster. Try stocking your kitchen with easy meals for busy days. And if you love restaurant food, challenge yourself to recreate your favorite dishes at home. You'll save money and maybe discover a hidden culinary talent!

3. Meal Planning

Plan your meals ahead. It reduces food waste and prevents last-minute takeout. Plus, it's healthier!

4. Cut Unnecessary Subscriptions

Review your subscriptions—streaming services, magazines, gym memberships. Cancel what you don't use regularly.

5. Shop Smarter

Before buying, ask: Do I really need this? Can I find it cheaper elsewhere? Impulse buys add up.

6. Reduce Utility Costs

Turn off lights when not needed, unplug devices, and consider energy-efficient appliances.

Allocate Funds Toward Debt Repayment

Once you've freed up some cash, allocate it toward paying off debt. Set a monthly goal above the minimum payments. The more you put toward debt, the faster you'll become debt-free. Remember, it's progress, not perfection!

5 NEGOTIATING WITH CREDITORS

Negotiating with creditors can be a challenging but essential process, especially when you're dealing with debt. Let's break down the key points you've mentioned:

1. **Understanding Your Rights as a Debtor**: It's crucial to know your rights when dealing with creditors. Here are some fundamental rights you should be aware of:

    o **Fair Debt Collection Practices Act (FDCPA)**: This federal law protects consumers from abusive or unfair debt collection practices. It outlines rules that debt collectors must follow, such as not harassing you, not calling at unreasonable hours, and providing accurate information.

- **Validation of Debt**: You have the right to request validation of the debt. If a creditor contacts you, you can ask for written proof that the debt is legitimate.

- **Cease and Desist**: You can send a cease-and-desist letter to stop collection calls if they become harassing. However, this won't make the debt go away; it just stops the calls.

2. **Negotiation Techniques**: When negotiating with creditors, keep these tips in mind:

    - **Be Prepared**: Understand your financial situation thoroughly. Know how much you can realistically pay.

    - **Communicate**: Reach out to your creditors proactively. Explain your situation honestly and ask if they're willing to negotiate.

- **Offer a Settlement**: Propose a lump-sum payment that's less than the total debt. Creditors may accept if they believe it's the best they can get.

- **Be Persistent and Polite**: Negotiations might take time. Stay patient and maintain a respectful tone.

3. **Addressing Collection Calls and Letters**:

- **Calls**: If you receive collection calls, stay calm. Ask for the caller's name, company, and mailing address. Request that they communicate in writing.

- **Letters**: When you receive collection letters, read them carefully. Some may contain important information about your rights or options.

Now, let's talk about the DIY approach. While some people hire debt settlement companies, you can handle this on your own. Here's why:

- **Benefits of DIY Debt Settlement**:

    - **Cost Savings**: By negotiating directly, you avoid the fees charged by professional settlement companies.

    - **Control**: You decide the timing and approach.

    - **Better Results**: Some experts believe that DIY negotiations can yield better outcomes.

However, there are downsides:

- **Tax Implications**: If a significant amount of debt is forgiven, you may owe taxes on the forgiven portion.

- **Credit Score Impact**: Settlements will negatively affect your credit score and remain on your report for seven years.

- **Self-Reliance**: You won't have a professional negotiating on your behalf.

Remember, each situation is unique, so consider seeking legal advice or credit counseling if needed. And most importantly, take care of yourself during this process!

6 EMERGENCY FUND

Let's dive into the world of emergency funds and how they can be your financial superhero when unexpected expenses come knocking at your door.

The Importance of Having an Emergency Fund

An **emergency fund** is like a financial safety net—a stash of cash set aside specifically for those "uh-oh" moments life throws our way. Here's why it matters:

1. **Unforeseen Expenses**: Life is full of surprises—some delightful, like finding a $20 bill in your old jeans pocket, and others less so, like sudden medical bills, car repairs, or unexpected home appliance breakdowns. An emergency fund acts as your buffer against these financial curveballs.

2. **Avoiding Debt**: Imagine this: Your car engine decides to stage a protest, and you're faced with a hefty repair bill. Without an emergency fund, you might resort to whipping out the credit card or taking out a high-interest loan. But having that cushion of cash means you won't have to borrow and pay interest. It's like telling debt, "Not today, my friend!"

3. **Peace of Mind**: Knowing you have a financial safety net can help you sleep better at night. It's like having a cozy blanket of security wrapped around you. Whether it's a job loss, unexpected medical expenses, or a leaky roof, you'll have the peace of mind that you're prepared.

Steps to Build an Emergency Fund While Paying Off Debt

Creating an emergency fund while tackling debt might feel like juggling flaming torches, but fear not—I've got some practical steps for you:

1. **Create a Budget**: Start by understanding your financial landscape. List all your debts, their interest rates, and minimum monthly payments. Then, create a budget that allocates a portion of your income toward both debt repayment and emergency savings[1]. Remember, every dollar counts!

2. **Start Small**: You don't need to summon a mountain of cash overnight. Begin with a modest goal, like saving $500. Once you hit that milestone, keep going. The ultimate aim is to have three to six months' worth of living expenses tucked away.

3. **Open a High-Yield Savings Account**: Your emergency fund should be easily accessible, but not too tempting. A high-yield savings account is ideal—it offers a decent interest rate while keeping your money liquid. Separate it from your daily-use account to avoid accidental withdrawals.

4. **Set Up Automatic Deposits**: Treat your emergency fund like a VIP guest. Set up automatic transfers from your paycheck or checking account. Consistency is key!

5. **Pay Down Your Debt Concurrently**: Yes, you can do both! While saving, continue making minimum payments on your debts. Some experts recommend a 50/30/20 budget: allocate 50% to needs (like housing and groceries), 30% to wants, and 20% to savings and debt repayment.

6. **Track Your Progress**: Celebrate each milestone. As your emergency fund grows, you'll feel more secure.

7. **Save Windfalls**: Unexpected bonuses, tax refunds, or birthday cash? Channel them straight into your emergency fund.

8. **Cash Back Rewards**: If you have a cash back credit card, consider directing those rewards into your fund. It's like turning your shopping sprees into financial padding.

How an Emergency Fund Prevents Future Debt

Think of your emergency fund as a superhero cape. When life throws a financial crisis your way, you don't have to rely on credit cards or loans. Instead, you swoop in with your cash reserves and save the day. No debt, no drama!

Remember, building an emergency fund is a journey. Start small, stay consistent, and watch your financial resilience grow. You've got this!

7 FRUGAL HABITS

Let's dive into lifestyle adjustments, frugal habits, and the fascinating psychology behind spending and impulse buying. Plus, I'll sprinkle in some inspiring success stories to keep things interesting.

Frugal Habits: Small Steps, Big Savings

1. Meat-Savvy Shopping
Bernadette Joy, a self-made millionaire, swears by this one: She buys the least expensive cuts of meat. Yep, she's the person meticulously comparing chicken prices at the grocery store. For example, when she craves Korean barbecue, she

opts for the more budget-friendly end-cuts of beef short-ribs. They might not be as pretty, but they're easier on her wallet and just as delicious.

2. Hotel Vanity Kits: More Than Just Travel Souvenirs

Next time you stay in a hotel, pay attention to those complimentary vanity kits. Bernadette Joy, the same frugal guru from earlier, saves hers. Those toothbrushes, toothpaste, and fancy combs? She repurposes them. The shower caps and hair elastics? Perfect for organizing chargers and converters. And yes, she's even used the extra toothbrushes to clean her shoes after a long walking tour. Talk about resourcefulness!

3. Repurposing Takeout Containers

Remember those old margarine and cool whip containers your parents used for leftovers? Well, today's takeout containers are fancier, but the principle remains. Instead of tossing them, reuse them for storage. They come in various sizes and are sturdier than traditional plastic tubs. So, whether you're storing last night's pad thai or organizing small items around the house, those containers have your back.

The Psychology of Spending and Impulse Buying

Why Do We Splurge?

Impulse buying—oh, that siren call of instant gratification! Our brains light up like a Christmas tree when we make a purchase. It's all about dopamine—the feel-good neurotransmitter. But here's the twist: That fleeting happiness can later turn into regret when we realize we didn't really need that third novelty mug or the sparkly unicorn-shaped lamp. Oops!

What Motivates Impulse Buying?

1. **Social Status and Image**: Impulse buyers often want to look good in the eyes of others. That shiny new purchase? It's a status symbol.

2. **Emotional Control (or Lack Thereof)**: Impulse buyers struggle with managing emotions. Anxiety? Check. Difficulty resisting emotional urges? Double-check.

3. **Happiness Quest**: Some buy to improve their mood. Feeling down? Maybe a new gadget will fix it!

4. **Consequences? Nah!**: Impulse buyers don't always consider the aftermath. They just want it now.

Inspiring Debt-Free Living Stories

1. **BudgetGirl Pays Off $33K in Debt on a Low Income**: This real-life superhero tackled debt head-on, proving that frugality isn't just for the wealthy.

2. **A Debt-Free Christmas & New Life**: Imagine celebrating the holidays without financial stress. It's possible!

3. **Gratefully Debt Free**: These success stories show that with determination and smart choices, you can break free from debt's grip.

Remember, every small frugal step counts. Whether it's saving on meat, repurposing hotel goodies, or resisting that impulse buy, you're on your way to financial freedom!

Let's delve into these inspiring debt-free stories.

1. **BudgetGirl Pays Off $33K in Debt on a Low Income**:

    o **Who is BudgetGirl?** Her real name is Sara Wilson, and she's a financial influencer who documented her journey to debt freedom on YouTube. Despite a modest salary as a newspaper reporter, she managed to pay off a whopping $33,000 in student loans within just three years.

    o **How did she do it?** Sara combined several strategies: budgeting rigorously, side hustling, and maintaining a frugal lifestyle. She hustled away debt by blogging, doing surveys, and even working part-time at Starbucks. Her determination and smart choices paved the way for her success.

    o **Takeaway**: Budgeting and resourcefulness can make a significant impact, even when your income isn't sky-high. Sara's story reminds us that anyone can achieve debt freedom with the right mindset and persistence.

2. **A Debt-Free Christmas & New Life**:

    o   Imagine a holiday season without the weight of financial stress. That's precisely what some people experience after becoming debt-free. By diligently managing their finances, they break free from the shackles of debt and create a new life.

    o   **How does it work?** These debt-free individuals prioritize saving, budgeting, and making intentional choices. Instead of relying on credit cards or loans during the holidays, they plan ahead, set realistic budgets, and find joy in simple celebrations.

    o   **Takeaway**: Being debt-free isn't just about numbers; it's about reclaiming peace of mind and enjoying life without constant financial worry. A debt-free Christmas becomes a gift in itself.

3. **Gratefully Debt Free**:

    - Some years ago, a family found themselves in a place of gratitude after becoming debt-free. They credit their financial turnaround to the resources they discovered—perhaps similar to the ones you're exploring now.

    - **What did they learn?** Outside of their salvation, marriage, and children, being debt-free became the best thing that ever happened to them. It's a testament to the transformative power of financial freedom.

    - **Takeaway**: Gratitude accompanies debt freedom. It's not just about the absence of debt; it's about gaining control, reducing stress, and appreciating the simple joys of life.

Remember, these stories aren't just about money—they're about resilience, choices, and the human spirit. Whether you're paying off debt or dreaming of a debt-free future, know that you're not alone. Many have walked this path before you, and their stories inspire us all.

8 EXTRA INCOME

Let's dive into the world of side hustles and extra income. Whether you're looking to pay off debt, save up for a special goal, or simply boost your financial well-being, there are plenty of opportunities out there. Here's a concise rundown of some side hustle ideas and how they can help you:

1. **Freelancing**: Freelancing is a classic way to earn extra money. Whether you're a graphic designer, writer, editor, or website developer, there's demand for your skills. Platforms like Fiverr, Upwork, and Freelancer.com connect you with clients, making it easier to find projects.

2. **Pet Sitting and Doggie Day Care**: If you're an animal lover, consider pet sitting or offering doggie day care services. People are always looking for reliable caregivers for their furry friends.

3. **Dog Walking**: Combine exercise with earning money by becoming a dog walker. It's a win-win—you stay active, and the pups get their daily stroll.

4. **Tech Setup Services**: Help less tech-savvy individuals set up their gadgets, troubleshoot issues, or optimize their devices.

5. **Blogging**: If you enjoy writing, start a blog. Monetize it through ads, affiliate marketing, or sponsored content.

6. **Senior Sitting and Companion**: Spend time with seniors who appreciate companionship. You might assist with errands, meal preparation, or just be a friendly presence.

7. **Babysitting and Child Care**: Babysitting isn't just for teenagers. Many parents need reliable childcare during evenings or weekends.

8. **Virtual Assistant**: Offer administrative support remotely. Tasks can include scheduling, email management, and data entry.

9. **Mobile Car Washing and Detailing**: Turn your car-cleaning skills into a side gig. Offer mobile car wash services to busy professionals.

10. **Local Handyman**: If you're handy with tools, offer your services for small home repairs or maintenance tasks.

Remember, side hustles allow you to explore potential business ideas with minimal upfront costs and time commitments. Now, let's talk about how extra income accelerates debt payoff:

- **Debt Paydown Acceleration**: When you have additional income from side hustles, you can allocate it directly toward paying off your debts. This approach helps you tackle the principal amount without accumulating more interest. Imagine paying down your credit card balance faster because you're earning extra cash on the side!

If you're curious about specific numbers and personalized payment plans, you might want to try a debt payoff calculator. Websites like Bankrate offer tools that create customized plans based on your income, debts, and interest rates[1]. Remember, every little bit counts, so whether it's a few extra dollars from a side gig or a substantial freelance project, it all contributes to your financial progress.

9 STRATEGIES

Let's delve into the world of debt repayment and explore both practical strategies and the emotional landscape. Whether you're tackling student loans, credit card balances, or any other form of debt, it's essential to navigate this journey with clarity and resilience. Here we go!

Common Mistakes in Debt Repayment

1. Being Too Hard on Yourself

Debt can feel like a personal failing, but it's crucial to recognize that over-indebtedness affects many people. Low income and lack of financial resources often play a more significant role than willpower. <u>So, cut yourself some slack and focus on solutions</u>

2. Not Taking Advantage of Help

You don't have to face debt alone. Nonprofit credit counseling services exist to provide personalized assistance. They can help you set up a plan for managing and eliminating your debts. <u>Look into organizations like the National Foundation for Credit Counseling (NFCC)</u>

3. Neglecting Financial Literacy

Understanding finance matters. Research shows that low-income individuals with better money management skills tend to have lower debt-to-income ratios. Educate yourself about personal finance to make informed decisions.

The Emotional Aspects of Debt Repayment

Debt isn't just about numbers; it's also about emotions. Here's how psychology impacts borrowers:

1. Anxiety and Stress

Borrowing money often triggers anxiety. The fear of accumulating debt, meeting financial obligations, and facing long-term consequences can take a toll on mental well-being. If you're new to borrowing or facing financial difficulties, this stress can be overwhelming,

2. Desire and Gratification

On the flip side, borrowing can evoke feelings of desire and immediate gratification. People borrow to achieve life goals—buying a home, pursuing education, or starting a business. These aspirations can be powerful motivators, but they also come with emotional complexities.

3. Shame and Guilt

Struggling to repay debts can lead to feelings of shame and guilt. It's essential to recognize that debt doesn't define your worth. Seek support and focus on solutions rather than self-blame.

Strategies to Stay Motivated

Paying off debt is a marathon, not a sprint. Here are some practical ways to stay motivated:

1. **Remember the "Why"**: Regularly remind yourself why you're paying off debt. Whether it's financial freedom, future goals, or escaping interest payments, keep

your motivation alive.

2. **Get Organized**: Create a clear plan. Prioritize high-interest debts, consider consolidation, and set achievable milestones. Having a roadmap makes the journey less daunting.

3. **Accountability Partner**: Share your debt repayment journey with someone—a friend, family member, or even an online community. Accountability keeps you on track.

4. **Celebrate Small Wins**: Each debt milestone deserves recognition. Treat yourself (within reason) when you hit a goal. Maybe a celebratory date night or a small indulgence.

5. **Visualize Your Progress**: Use a vision board or a simple spreadsheet to track your progress. Seeing how far you've come can boost motivation.

Remember, you're not alone in this journey. Many have successfully paid off debt, and you can too

10 FINANCIAL DISCIPLINE

Let's dive into the world of financial discipline.

What Is Financial Discipline? Financial discipline, also known as money discipline, involves setting specific financial goals and tracking your progress toward achieving them. It's about creating habits that allow you to take control of your money, build savings, and work toward a stable financial future[1]. Think of it as your financial GPS—helping you stay on course even when there are tempting detours (like those concert tickets or new shoes).

Here are **seven essential steps** to achieve financial discipline:

1. **Getting Clear About Financial Goals**: Start by setting clear financial objectives. Write down short-term, mid-term, and long-term goals. Whether it's saving for a vacation, paying off debt, or investing for retirement, having specific targets helps you stay focused and motivated.

2. **Creating a Convenient Budget**: A budget is your roadmap. Track your income and expenses, allocate funds for necessities, savings, and discretionary spending. Regularly review your budget to ensure you're staying within your limits.

3. **Paying Down Existing Debt**: Debt can weigh you down. Prioritize paying off high-interest debts (like credit cards) to free up more money for savings and investments.

4. **Opening a High-Yield Savings Account**: A dedicated savings account with a competitive interest rate can help your money grow faster. Automate regular contributions to build an emergency fund and save for your goals.

5. **Establishing an Emergency Fund**: Life throws curveballs, so having an emergency fund is crucial. Aim for 3–6 months' worth of living expenses in a separate account. It provides peace of mind and prevents you from dipping into other savings when unexpected expenses arise.

6. **Cutting Back on Spending**: Be mindful of your spending habits. Identify areas where you can trim unnecessary expenses. Small changes—like brewing your own coffee or cooking at home—add up over time.

7. **Seeking Sound Investment Strategies**: Once you've built a solid financial foundation, consider investing. Learn about different investment options (stocks, bonds, real estate, etc.) and choose strategies aligned with your risk tolerance and goals.

Remember, financial success is a marathon, not a sprint. Celebrate small victories along the way, and stay committed to your plan. Persistence pays off!

ABOUT THE AUTHOR

Arthur Crandon is a retired lawyer and a prolific writer. He is British and grew up in a rural community in Somerset. He has lived in England, Wales, Hong Kong and the Philippines and now spends most of his time in the Philippines with his Visayan wife and their son.

He loves to hear from anyone who has anything to do with the Philippines – you can email him anytime on:

ac@arthurcrandon.co.uk

www.ingramcontent.com/pod-product-compliance
Lightning Source LLC
Chambersburg PA
CBHW051535240526
45471CB00020B/2733